Writing

Grades 4-5

Y0-AGN-589

How to Get

BETTER TEST SCORES

on Standardized Tests

Perfection Learning®

CREDITS

Senior Editor: Terry Ofner
Editor: Judith A. Bates
Art Director: Randy Messer
Designer: Deborah Lea Bell
Cover Illustration: Michael A. Aspengren

SCHOOL ACKNOWLEDGMENTS

Fairmeadows Elementary School, West Des Moines, Iowa
Madrid Elementary School, Madrid, Iowa

©1998 Perfection Learning® Corporation
1000 North Second Avenue, P.O. Box 500, Logan, Iowa 51546-1099
Tel: 1-800-831-4190 • Fax: 1-712-644-2392
ISBN 0-7891-2349-5
Printed in the U.S.A.

TABLE OF CONTENTS

What Is the Purpose of an Essay Test?

There are many different ways to test a student's knowledge. For example, you may have taken a test that measured your basic skills. Perhaps you have done a book-related project or written a book report that was graded. You have probably taken multiple-choice and true/false tests in social studies or science. A writing test is a little different from all of these.

A writing test measures how well you express your thoughts "on demand." On demand means that you don't know what you will write about ahead of time. Some writing tests ask you to write a letter. Others may have you create a report. Still others may want you to write an article for the school newspaper. But most writing tests ask you to write an essay. Essay writing is the subject of this book. (For information on other types of writing tests, see page 31.)

In essay writing, you express what you think about a subject. All essays include the following.

- **The introduction** is the first paragraph of the essay. It introduces the subject. It also contains the central idea.

- **The body** follows the introduction. There can be one or more body paragraphs. Each paragraph provides facts, reasons, and/or examples that support the central idea.

- **The conclusion** is the last paragraph. It provides an ending for the essay. This paragraph also sums up your thoughts.

To help remember the parts of an essay, look at the figure below.

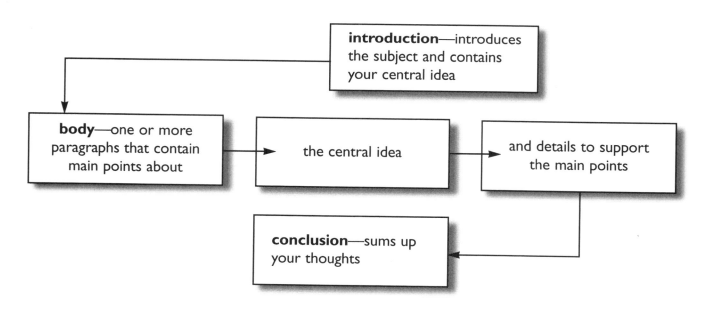

How Will My Essay Be Graded?

Your essay will be scored by test readers. Test readers are trained to look for certain standards in your writing. Here are the standards a test reader might look for.

- focus—how well your essay relates to the central idea
- organization—the way in which you present your ideas
- support—the details you offer to back up your central idea
- conventions—how well you follow the rules of the English language

Test readers often use rubrics to score student writing. A *rubric* is a set of special standards. Listed below are the standards a test reader might use for a rubric.

- The essay has a beginning, middle, and end.
- The essay has a clear central idea.
- The essay answers the prompt (the writing assignment) clearly and completely.
- The essay stays focused on the central idea.
- The essay offers enough support for the central idea.
- The essay follows the rules of sentence writing. It contains a variety of sentence lengths and styles.
- The essay follows the rules of punctuation, spelling, and grammar.

Why Do I Need This Book?

This book will show you how to get your thoughts down on paper quickly and clearly. You will see how other students responded to test prompts. In addition, you will practice writing the most common types of essays. Test-taking tips and writing strategies throughout this book will help you write the best essay possible. There's even a section on the most common problems in essay writing. It will show you how to avoid these problems. In short, this book will teach you how to get your essay right *the first time*.

How to READ A PROMPT

A *prompt* is the assignment for a writing test. The prompt gives you directions on what to write. It also sets up the subject of your essay. It helps if you know how to read the prompt for clues. These clues are found in key words and phrases.

Noting Key Words and Phrases

Read the prompt for Ty's essay test. Notice the key words and phrases he underlined. These helped Ty find the central idea.

Prompt

> The city council is thinking about passing a new law. It would <u>ban the use of bikes, in-line skates, and skateboards on public sidewalks. Decide how you feel</u> about this idea. Then <u>write an essay. State your opinion.</u> Then <u>support it with convincing reasons</u>. Be sure to <u>explain your reasons</u> in detail.

The prompt tells Ty how to set up his essay. He is to tell whether he agrees or disagrees with the city council's idea. Then he is to give reasons why he feels as he does.

The prompt also provides Ty with words or phrases that tell him what to include. The key phrase *explain your reasons* tells Ty exactly what to do. He will support his central idea with facts, examples, and/or reasons. He may also want to include certain phrases such as *ban the use of bikes* or *public sidewalks* in his central idea.

Read the prompt below. Underline the key words or phrases that might be helpful to a writer.

Prompt

People live in the country, small or large towns, or big cities. Think about where you live or places you have visited. Choose one place where you would like to live. Explain why you think it is best. Be sure to give specific details.

As you continue through this book, use the steps in the Test-Taking Tip on this page to help you find the subject of a prompt.

The ESSAY TO EXPLAIN

When you write an essay that compares small towns with big cities, you are writing to explain. You are also writing to explain when you write how to do something. In an *essay to explain*, you are expected to provide information or explain a subject. This type of essay is often called *expository* writing.

Parts of an essay to explain

- introduction
- body
- conclusion

The *introduction* of an essay to explain introduces your subject. It states your central idea. It also makes the reader want to read the rest of the essay. (See the Strategy of Good Writing sidebar on this page.) The *central idea* in an essay to explain is a fact or opinion that you will support. Below is an example of a central idea.

Central idea
Farming is an important industry.

The *body* contains one or more paragraphs. It supports your central idea. Think about the example above. The body of an essay based on that central idea would provide details that support the idea that farming is an important industry.

The *conclusion* sums up your essay. It also ends with a strong thought. This leaves your readers thinking about your ideas.

Words you might find in a prompt for an essay to explain

compare	discuss	summarize
contrast	explain	tell
define	propose	

Strategy OF GOOD WRITING

GETTING YOUR READERS' ATTENTION

A good writer opens an essay with a "hook." A hook is a sentence that grabs the readers' attention. You may have some ideas of your own for hooking readers. If not, several types of hooks are listed below.

- **Surprise your readers.** Shock them with a fact. Or provide them with a startling description.

- **Entertain your readers.** Tell them an interesting story that has to do with your subject.

- **Challenge your readers.** Ask them a question. Or invite them to solve a problem. You might even give them a command.

- **Make your readers think.** Begin with a strong statement, quote, or saying.

continued

Below is an example of an essay prompt that Danielle was given on a writing test.

Prompt

Boys and girls often say, "I <u>can't wait</u> until I'm <u>old enough</u> to _____."
Write an essay <u>telling</u> about something you cannot wait until you are
old enough to do.

Getting Started

Look at the figure below. Danielle created it to help her organize her
ideas. Notice that she placed the subject in the center circle. She listed
supporting ideas in the circles around it.

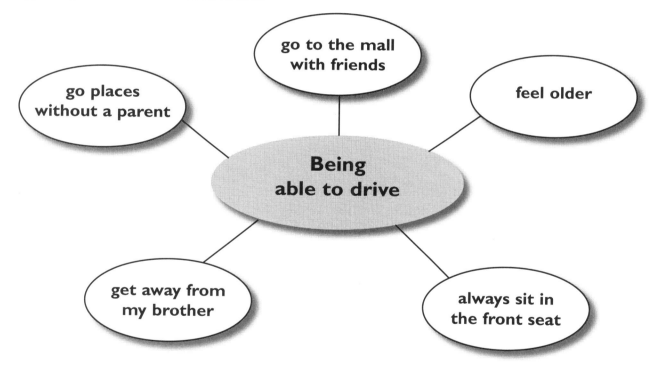

As you read Danielle's essay on the next page,
look for proof of the preplanning she did.

DANIELLE'S ESSAY

I can't do **this** by myself! I can't go **there** by myself! I can't wait until I'm old enough to drive. Then I will be able to go where I want and do what I want without a parent.

I want to be able to go to the mall with my friends without an adult tagging along. I want to feel like I'm older and not a little kid. I want to be able to talk with my friends without being interrupted by my parents. If I could drive, I could do these things.

I want to be able to get away from my brother. I don't want to fight over the front seat with him either. We would both be happier if I could drive.

My point is that I don't want to be trapped by my family. I want to be able to go places without them. That's the reason I can't wait to drive.

Looking at DANIELLE'S ESSAY

• Does Danielle's introduction grab your attention? Why or why not?

• Locate Danielle's central idea. Does it clearly show the subject of the prompt? Does it show Danielle's ideas about the subject?

• Does the body support the main points of the central idea?

• Has Danielle included enough support in the body? If not, what kinds of details might she have added?

• Does the conclusion sum up Danielle's thoughts about the subject?

• How effective is Danielle's ending?

continued

On Your Own

Now it's your turn to write an essay to explain. Read the prompt below. Then underline the key words and phrases.

Prompt

> Everyone has jobs or chores. Before you begin writing, think about why you do one of your jobs or chores. Now explain what your job or chore is and why you do it.

Now use the blank figure below to organize your ideas. Refer to the figure as you write your essay. (See the Test-Taking Tip on this page for help in narrowing down your ideas.)

When you finish writing, use the rubric on the next page to score your essay. Fill in the appropriate circle for each standard in the Score column (*1* is the lowest; *5* is the highest).

Time Allowed

minutes

Test-Taking TIP

NARROWING DOWN YOUR IDEAS QUICKLY

When narrowing down your ideas into a central idea, think about the following.

- Select the ideas you know the most about. They will be the easiest to support.

- Select the most important ideas. Weak ideas make a weak paper.

- Select ideas your audience will be familiar with. Readers will find it easier to understand ideas they know something about. You can avoid long explanations by using familiar ideas.

Rubric	Score (*1* is the lowest; *5* is the highest)
The introduction grabs the readers' attention.	① ② ③ ④ ⑤
The introduction includes a clear central idea.	① ② ③ ④ ⑤
The body offers several details to support my central idea.	① ② ③ ④ ⑤
The conclusion sums up my essay.	① ② ③ ④ ⑤
The essay ends with a strong thought. It will leave my readers thinking about my ideas.	① ② ③ ④ ⑤
The essay uses the rules of written English.	① ② ③ ④ ⑤

Consider This

1. Look at the rubric. What are your strengths? What are your weaknesses?

   _____

   _____

2. If you were a test reader, would you find the essay interesting? If not, what could you do to make it more appealing?

   _____

   _____

Strategy OF GOOD WRITING

DEALING WITH CON PARAGRAPHS

• Why would you include reasons that are against your own? The best way to win an argument is to begin by agreeing with the person you are arguing with. Con paragraphs do just that. They tell your readers that you are a well-informed person. You are able to see both sides of an issue.

• A good writer places a con paragraph first in the body. This strategy draws in readers who might disagree with the central idea.

• A good writer states his or her strongest pro statement just before the conclusion. Then your reader is more likely to agree with your ideas.

The ESSAY TO PERSUADE

When you try to convince your friend to play a game, you are being persuasive. You are also persuasive when you give reasons to your parents about why you should spend the night with a friend. In an *essay to persuade*, you are expected to state an opinion. Then you must try to convince your readers to agree with you. This type of essay is often called *persuasive* writing.

Parts of an essay to persuade

- introduction
- body
- conclusion

The *introduction* of an essay to persuade introduces your subject. It also states your central idea. The central idea is a statement of your opinion. For example, suppose your local school board is considering a plan to continue school through the summer months. Below are two examples of central ideas.

I am in favor of continuing school during the summer.

I believe that school should not be continued during the summer.

The *body* contains one or more paragraphs. It states reasons that support your opinion. Any reason you offer that supports your opinion is a *pro*. *Pro paragraphs* support your opinion, whether you are for or against an idea. See the "Dealing with Con Paragraphs" sidebar on this page for more details.

Some writers include a con paragraph in their essays. *Con paragraphs* give reasons against your opinion.

The *conclusion* begins by restating your central idea. An effective conclusion ends with a strong thought that leaves your readers thinking about your ideas.

Words you might find in a prompt for an essay to persuade

agree, disagree	issue	position
argue, argument	opinion	should, should not
consider	oppose	support
convince	persuade	viewpoint
debate		

Below is an example of an essay prompt that Erin was given on a writing test.

Prompt

Your local school board is thinking about <u>making students wear school uniforms</u>. The board members have asked for the <u>opinions</u> of all students before making a decision. <u>Write an essay persuading</u> the school board members to agree with your opinion.

Getting Started

First Erin decided whether she was for or against wearing uniforms. Then she organized her ideas about the issue. Look at the chart that Erin created for the above prompt. Notice that she placed her opinion—that she is *for* wearing school uniforms—at the top of the chart. Then she listed the pros and cons in separate columns. Reminder: Since Erin is *for* wearing school uniforms, any argument *for* wearing uniforms is a pro. Any argument *not in favor of* wearing uniforms is a con.

Issue: wearing school uniforms
My Position: for

Pros	Cons
don't have enough money for brand-name clothing	students have no way to express themselves
no worries about whether clothing is "cool" enough	students should have the right to make their own choices
would help parents' clothing bill	everyone would look the same
would be more presentable	
save time choosing what to wear	

Look for proof of the preplanning Erin did as you read her essay on the next page.

continued

ERIN'S ESSAY

Looking at ERIN'S ESSAY

• Does Erin's introduction grab your attention? Why or why not?

• Locate Erin's central idea. Is her opinion on wearing school uniforms clearly stated?

• Locate Erin's con paragraph. Are the details she offers related to the subject? If not, what might she have added?

Do you pay attention to what others wear? Do you wish you had clothes like theirs? Many students do. That's why I think wearing uniforms to school is a good idea.

I understand that some people feel that wearing school uniforms doesn't allow students to express themselves. Others think that everyone would look the same if they wore uniforms.

However, I feel that wearing school uniforms would solve a number of problems that occur in schools every day. Having school uniforms would stop those problems that occur when students don't have enough money to buy brand-name clothing. How many times have you heard parents complain about the price of clothing? Mine do all the time. Brand-name clothes are expensive. But many students think they are the only "cool" stuff to wear. Some students are teased because they don't have brand-name clothes.

School uniforms could help in other ways too. They would look more presentable than some of the T-shirts students wear. Many T-shirts advertise beer or cigarettes. If everyone wore school uniforms, teachers wouldn't have to send students home or be embarrassed when a visitor comes to class.

Uniforms could change a lot of people's lives. Each morning, many students have a

THE ESSAY TO PERSUADE

hard time finding the right clothes to wear. They don't want to be teased if they wear the wrong outfit. Or they don't want to be embarrassed because their clothes are old and out of style. I would rather wear the same outfit every day than waste 30 minutes every morning choosing clothes. I could use this time for chores, extra studying, or reading.

I believe that the school board should decide to have students wear uniforms. Teachers and parents would be happier. And in the long run, students would be happier too.

Looking at ERIN'S ESSAY

- Locate Erin's pro paragraphs. Has she provided strong details related to the subject? If not, what kinds of details might she have added?

- Does Erin restate her opinion in the conclusion?

- How effective is Erin's ending?

On Your Own

Now it's your turn to write an essay to persuade. Read the prompt below. Then underline key words and phrases.

Prompt

Some school districts in the United States feel that boys and girls are not treated equally in all subject areas. Therefore, they have created all-male and all-female classes in the elementary schools. Think about the issue. State your opinion and then persuade a friend.

Now decide whether you are for or against all-male and all-female classrooms. Then use the blank chart below to list your pros and cons. Refer to the chart as you write your essay.

When you finish writing, apply the rubric on the next page to your essay. Fill in the appropriate circle for each standard in the Score column (*1* is the lowest; *5* is the highest).

Time Allowed

minutes

Issue: My Position:	
Pros	**Cons**

Test-Taking
TIP

SELECTING YOUR PROS AND CONS QUICKLY

When trying to decide which pros and cons to include in your essay, think about the following.

- Include the strongest arguments in favor of your opinion in your pro paragraphs. For example, you may feel that girls should not be allowed to play football on all-male teams. For this subject, your strongest pro might be that male players would not play their best for fear of hurting the girls. Another strong pro would be that many girls are not as physically strong as boys.

- If you include a con paragraph, use the strongest argument against your opinion. Your readers will see that you're not afraid to state an opposing idea.

Rubric	Score (*1* is the lowest; *5* is the highest)
The introduction includes a clear central idea that states my opinion.	① ② ③ ④ ⑤
If I have included a con paragraph, it states arguments against my opinion.	① ② ③ ④ ⑤
The con paragraph contains enough support.	① ② ③ ④ ⑤
I have included one or more pro paragraphs stating arguments that support my opinion.	① ② ③ ④ ⑤
The pro paragraphs contain enough support.	① ② ③ ④ ⑤
The conclusion paragraph restates my central idea.	① ② ③ ④ ⑤
The essay ends with a strong thought. It will leave my readers thinking about my ideas.	① ② ③ ④ ⑤
The essay follows the rules of written English.	① ② ③ ④ ⑤

Consider This

1. Based on the rubric, what are your strengths? What are your weaknesses?

   _____

   _____

2. If you were a test reader, would you be persuaded to agree with your opinion? If not, what could you do to make your essay more convincing?

   _____

   _____

Strategy OF GOOD WRITING

CENTRAL IDEA— NARRATIVE ESSAY

The central idea of an essay to tell a story can be a direct statement of what your essay will focus on.

Example: *My most embarrassing moment was when I tripped on the stage steps during an awards program.*

Or the central idea might simply be suggested in the introduction.

Example: *My gymnastics center was holding an awards program. I thought that I had done poorly at the meet. When my name was called, everyone cheered and applauded. I was so surprised that I almost fell out of my seat. That probably would have been better than what really happened.*

The important thing to remember is that by the time your readers finish the first paragraph, they should know what your paper will be about.

The ESSAY TO TELL A STORY

When you tell your friends about something that happened to you, you are telling a story. In an *essay to tell a story*, you are usually expected to relate an event from your personal life or create a fictional story. This type of essay is often called a *narrative* essay.

Parts of an essay to tell a story

- introduction
- body
- conclusion

The *introduction* of an essay to tell a story sets the stage. It introduces the characters and setting. The *setting* is the time and place the event took place. Also, this paragraph provides any background information your reader needs. Finally, your central idea should be included. For example, you are asked to tell about a time when you lost something. Your central idea might be, "Last year I lost my little sister at the mall."

The *body* contains one or more paragraphs. Some stories may need several paragraphs to explain. Others may require only one or two. The body should contain the main events of your story. You will want to arrange these events in time order. The *climax*, or most exciting part, of your story should also be included in the body.

The *conclusion* provides the ending for the story. This paragraph might also offer any thoughts you have about the experience. For example, you might tell what the experience taught you or how it changed you. A good conclusion ends with a strong thought that leaves your readers thinking about what you've written.

Words you might find in a prompt for an essay to tell a story

event	recall	story
experience	relate	tell
incident	remember	time
narrate		

Below is an example of an essay prompt that K. J. was given on a writing test. Look at the key words and phrases he underlined.

Prompt

Pretend that you and a friend found a map that shows <u>where a treasure is buried.</u> <u>Write a story telling about the adventure</u> you and your friend had trying to find the treasure.

Getting Started

K. J. began by mapping out his story. Look at the story map he created for the above prompt.

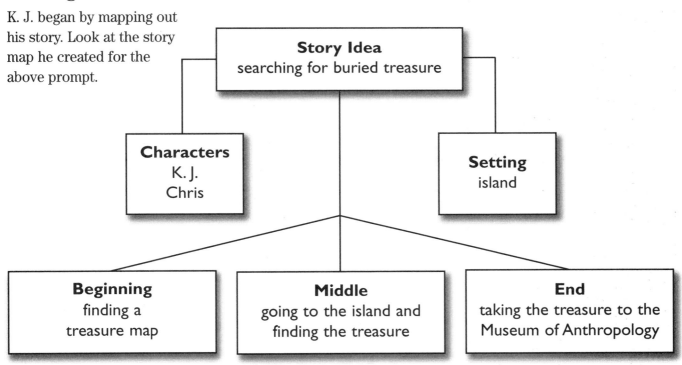

Look for proof of the preplanning K. J. did as you read his essay on the following page.

continued

K. J.'s Essay

Looking at K. J.'s Essay

- Does K. J.'s introduction grab your attention? Why or why not?

- Does K. J. introduce the characters? Does he give details about the setting in the first paragraph?

- Does he provide needed background knowledge?

- Does K. J.'s introduction tell what will happen in the story?

It all happened last year during fourth grade. One day after school, Chris and I were playing down at Witchacha Park. We were swinging and decided to go down the slide. So we jumped off our swings and started across the playground. Then, for no apparent reason, Chris tripped on something. It was a little metal box that was no bigger than a supply box. It was buried in the sand, so we dug it up. Carefully folded inside was a treasure map. We unfolded it and looked at it.

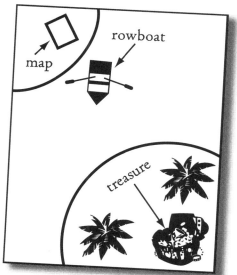

"How are we going to get to the island?" asked Chris.

"There is a rowboat right there," I said, pointing to the map. "But first we need to go home and get some shovels to dig up the treasure."

When we got back, we put the shovels in the boat and pushed off. We reached the island in no time.

"It's 4:30, and I'm hungry," Chris whined.

"First let's dig up the treasure. Then we'll go back to my house and grab a bite to eat."

The map showed that there were two palm trees on the island. The treasure was buried

between them. After two long hours of digging, there was a clank! We looked at each other.

Finally, Chris said, "It will take us at least an hour to get the treasure out of the hole. Won't our parents be getting worried?"

"No, because they went out to eat together," I assured him.

After an hour, we got the treasure out of the hole. We opened the big metal box. Our mouths fell open as we stared at the treasure.

Inside the box were gold coins, garnets, amethysts, bloodstones, and diamonds. There were also emeralds, pearls, rubies, sardonyxes, sapphires, opals, topazes, and turquoises. On top of the treasure, we saw a note. It read:

Congratulations! You have found the treasure of Captain Blackbeard. If you find my other treasures, you'll be sorry! I'll let this one go.

Signed, Captain Blackbeard

"That note gives me the creeps," Chris said.

"Me too," I answered.

Two weeks later, we took the treasure and gave it to the Museum of Anthropology. They offered us a one-billion-dollar reward!

Chris and I looked at each other, shrugged our shoulders, and said, "Sure!"

We donated the money to churches, schools, and charities. The museum asked us to tell our story. We told them it was a long story, but they didn't seem to mind.

"It all happened last year in fourth grade. Chris and I . . ."

Looking at K. J.'s Essay

- Label the beginning, middle, and end. Are the events organized in the order in which they happened?

- Does the conclusion provide an ending for the story?

continued

On Your Own

Now it's your turn to write an essay to tell a story. Read the prompt below. Then underline the key words and phrases.

Prompt

Something is happening around you all the time. Think about the past week. Write an eyewitness account of an event that happened on your way to or from school.

Now use the blank chart below to map out your story. Refer to the chart as you write your essay.

When you finish writing, apply the rubric on the next page to your essay. Fill in the appropriate circle for each standard in the Score column (*1* is the lowest; *5* is the highest).

Time Allowed

minutes

Strategy OF GOOD WRITING

MAKING YOUR STORY FLOW SMOOTHLY

As you write your story, use transitions to connect the events. Transitions are words and phrases that help the reader follow the order in which events happen. *First, then,* and *finally* are examples of transitions. Transitions should be as short and direct as possible.

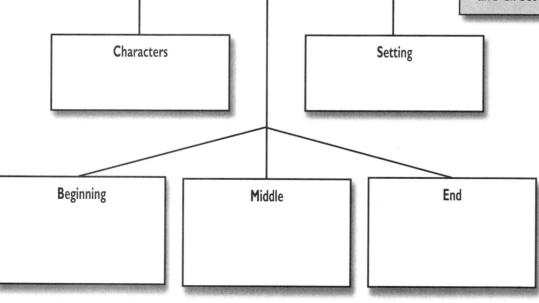

Story Idea

Characters

Setting

Beginning

Middle

End

Rubric	Score (*1* is the lowest; *5* is the highest)
The introduction provides background knowledge that readers need to understand the essay.	① ② ③ ④ ⑤
The central idea indicates what event my essay will be about.	① ② ③ ④ ⑤
The body contains the events of my story.	① ② ③ ④ ⑤
The events of my story are presented in the order in which they happened.	① ② ③ ④ ⑤
The conclusion provides an ending for my story.	① ② ③ ④ ⑤
The conclusion provides my thoughts about the event.	① ② ③ ④ ⑤
The essay ends with a strong thought that will leave my readers thinking about my story.	① ② ③ ④ ⑤
The essay follows the rules of written English.	① ② ③ ④ ⑤

Consider This

1. Based on the rubric, what are your strengths? What are your weaknesses?

   _____

   _____

2. If you were a test reader, do you think you would find it easy to follow what happened? Do you think you would find this story interesting? If not, what could you do to make your essay easier to follow and/or more interesting?

   _____

   _____

The ESSAY TO DESCRIBE

When you write your feelings in a journal or when you try to explain to a friend what your new dog looks like, you are being descriptive. In an *essay to describe* you are expected to *describe* a person, an object, or an event. Often this type of essay is called a *descriptive* essay.

Parts of an essay to describe

- introduction
- body
- conclusion

The *introduction* of an essay to describe introduces the subject. It also includes the central idea. Your central idea should present a general picture of your subject. For example, if you are writing to describe a sunrise, your central idea might read, "It was a sunrise that lifted the paints right from an artist's canvas."

The *body* of your essay can consist of any number of paragraphs. Some subjects may need several paragraphs to describe. Others may take only one or two. The body should provide details that create a picture in the readers' minds. These details should be arranged in a orderly manner. For example, from the first light of dawn to full daylight or from the front of the house to the back. For the sunrise example, your body would include details that allow your readers to see how colorful the sunrise was from beginning to end.

The *conclusion* restates your central idea. A good conclusion ends with a strong thought that leaves your readers thinking about your ideas.

Words you might find in a prompt for an essay to describe		
describe, description	in detail	smell
express	picture	taste
feel	see	tell
hear	senses	

Below is an example of a prompt Josh was given on a writing test. Look at the key words and phrases that he underlined.

Prompt

Pretend you are a space visitor from the planet Xearon. You have spent a day on Earth observing earthlings. <u>Write a journal account describing your experience on Earth</u>. Since your friends on Xearon don't know the names of objects on Earth, you must <u>describe the objects</u> without using their names.

Getting Started

Josh began by organizing his ideas about the subject. Look at the chart he created.

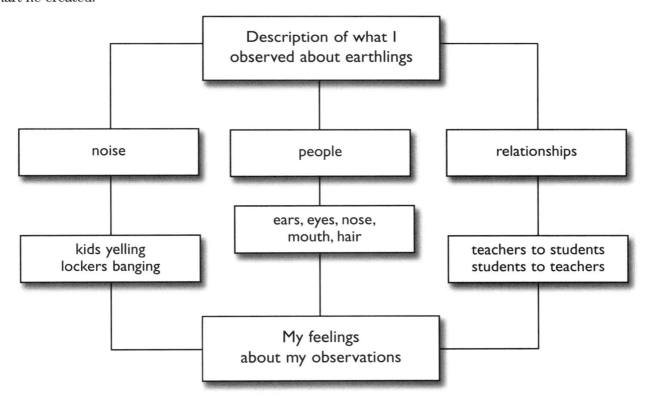

Look for the preplanning Josh did as you read his essay on the next page.

continued

JOSH'S ESSAY

Looking at JOSH'S ESSAY

- Does Josh's introduction grab your attention? Why or why not?

- Locate Josh's central idea. Does it state the subject clearly?

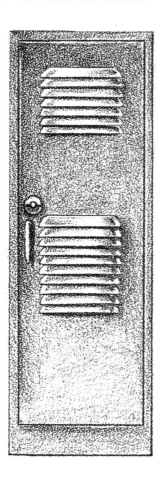

Report Xearth42

Earth. What an experience! I have been here for two periods of light and darkness. During this third light period, I am going to a place of learning. Here I will meet many earthlings. Maybe our questions will be answered about their inferior intelligence.

Report Xearth43

I have just fled the learning place called school. What a difficult experience. I will try to explain.

To begin with, the earthlings walked down a long hallway that was lined with metal boxes. These earthlings made some funny noises that sounded like "Hey, Dude!" "Hi!" "Get outta my way!" "Watch where you're going!" And lots of "Ha-ha-ha!" These might be forms of greeting, even though they are often accompanied by pushing and slapping backs. To make matters worse, the earthlings make these noises all at the same time. The noise of the voices and slamming of the doors on the metal boxes make a spaceship blastoff sound like a symphony.

Each metal box contained the treasures of the owner. One earthling placed its red, hooded warmer on a hook. I guess a warmer is only needed when an earthling goes outside in the icy wind. Then the earthling grabbed some learning tools and slammed the door. Oh, my poor ears!

Next, I followed the earthlings through an opening into a square area. Here there were

more earthlings. All earthlings have the same features, but the features vary in size, shape, and color. They are not like Xearonians at all.

On Xearon, we all look exactly alike. We are identified only by the symbol on our forward brain covering.

Earthlings all have a semicircular, protruding mass on each side of the forward brain covering. Set in the very front part of the brain covering are two marble-sized balls. These balls vary in color. Some earthlings have rich dirt-colored marbles while other marbles are the color of the liquid in our cleansing pools.

Between the marbles is another protruding feature. It is often long with two holes in the end. Sometimes this feature turns up, and sometimes it is pointy. These protrusions are quite unattractive.

Under the long protrusion is a slit. What a job it has! This slit is never still. It opens and closes when noises come from the interior of an earthling, which is quite often. Earthlings also fill the hole frequently with objects that are never seen again. When the objects are put into the hole, the slit closes, and the whole forward brain covering moves up and down.

Sometimes the slit is open. What a disgusting sight! The object in the hole is turned over and over by a pink snake. White

Looking at JOSH'S ESSAY

- Does the body of Josh's essay provide a picture of what a Xearonian might see?

- Underline details that appeal to the senses. What other details might Josh have included?

continued

**Looking at
JOSH'S ESSAY**

• How effective is Josh's ending?

grinding tools tear the object to pieces. Then the pieces disappear.

Earthlings all have a substance on the very top of their beings. Some earthlings must be embarrassed by the protrusions on their front-facing brain coverings. The substance is long, twisty or straight, and it covers the side protrusions. But other earthlings must be proud of their side protrusions because their substance is very short.

In the square area, the earthlings often sit and listen to an older earthling. This older one must be the leader. But the younger earthlings interrupt the leader with questions. How can they learn anything if they do not listen to what the leader says? The leader even lets the younger earthlings answer questions. If the leader does not know the answers, then it should not be the leader.

I observed until my brain was ready to explode. I fled the learning center and am now detailing the events for you, my superiors.

I have one final remark. GET ME OUT OF HERE!

On Your Own

Now it's your turn to write an essay to describe. Read the prompt below. Then underline the key words and phrases

Prompt

Describe either a very hot summer day or a bitterly cold winter day. Begin with the morning and imagine some of your activities during the day. Make your reader experience what you are describing.

Now use the blank chart below, or one of your choosing, to list your details and ideas about the day. Refer to the chart as you write your essay.

When you finish writing, apply the rubric on the next page to your essay. Fill in the appropriate circle for each standard in the Score column (*1* is the lowest; *5* is the highest).

Time Allowed

minutes

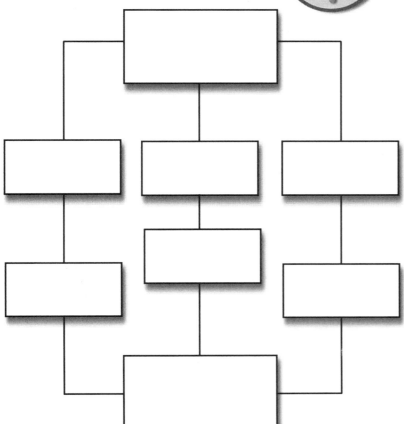

Test-Taking TIP

ORGANIZING YOUR DETAILS

- Your writing will go more quickly if you have a plan. Writing to describe usually shows where items are in relation to one another. For example, you might describe a school day from the first bell to the last bell or a house from top to bottom. Or you might begin a description of your bedroom by describing what's on the walls first. Then you would move toward the middle of the room.

- Once you choose your subject, picture it in your mind. Then ask yourself, "If someone were describing this object or event to me, how could he or she give the details so they would provide me with the clearest picture?" Once you have answered that question, you can begin writing quickly and easily.

continued

Rubric	Score (*1* is the lowest; *5* is the highest)
The introduction grabs the readers' attention.	① ② ③ ④ ⑤
The introduction includes a clear central idea.	① ② ③ ④ ⑤
The body includes enough details that use the senses. The readers will have a true sense of my subject.	① ② ③ ④ ⑤
The details are presented in an orderly way.	① ② ③ ④ ⑤
The conclusion restates my central idea.	① ② ③ ④ ⑤
The essay ends with a strong thought that will leave my readers thinking about my ideas.	① ② ③ ④ ⑤
The essay follows the rules of written English.	① ② ③ ④ ⑤

Consider This

1. Based on the rubric, what are your strengths? What are your weaknesses?

   _____

   _____

2. If you were the test reader, do you think you would get a clear picture of the subject of this essay? Do you think you would find the descriptions interesting? If not, what could you do as the writer to make your essay more clear and interesting?

   _____

   _____

Other Types
OF WRITING TESTS

Most writing tests will ask you to write an essay such as those discussed earlier. But some tests ask for different forms of writing. Some of those types of writing tests are listed below.

friendly letter
letter to a friend, relative, or someone else you know

business letter
a formal letter to a businessperson, a lawmaker, or another professional

letter to the editor
a formal letter that can be published in a newspaper. Normally the letter states an opinion on an issue.

report
an informational report based on a list of facts provided in the prompt

Most writing is either to explain, to persuade, to tell a story, or to describe. Therefore, you should be able to use the skills you've already learned when writing letters or reports. Read the examples that follow. Then select one of the prompts on page 37, and write an essay on your own.

FRIENDLY LETTER

Depending on the prompt, you could be asked to do any of the four types of writing in a friendly letter. Combine what you know about essay writing with the format of a friendly letter.

Read the prompt. Then see how the elements of both narrative and descriptive writing were used in the friendly letter that follows.

heading—writer's address and the date

greeting—tells whom the letter is to, followed by a comma

Prompt

It is the middle of summer. You and your family are vacationing in a cabin high in the mountains. Describe the area in a letter to a friend.

P.O. Box 1413
Spider Lake, WY 82011
August 8, 19—

Dear Eddie,

Awesome! That's the only way to describe the view from my bedroom window. At home, all I see from my window is the tan and brown house next door.

Trees are everywhere, swaying gently in the cool breeze. They are so tall and close together that they hide the sky in places. They smell like the fresh tree Dad brought home for Christmas last year. I've been collecting pine needles and pinecones in a jar. When I come home, I'll still be able to smell the mountain air.

body—the paragraphs that state the writer's ideas and thoughts

There's a place not far from the cabin where you can look out over the whole world. I can see the town at the foot of the mountain. The river looks like an old shoelace that was just dropped on the ground. I can't believe it's the same river that I tried to throw a rock across. The rock never even reached the middle of the river.

Up here, I don't have to listen to Mrs. Winters' dog howl all night. All I hear outside my window are crickets and an owl. It's so quiet that it was hard to fall asleep the first couple of nights we were here. But now I'm afraid I won't be able to sleep when we get back to the city. It's so noisy there.

The sky is clear blue. I guess I didn't know what the sky really looked like before. In the city, it is always kind of gray. Remember the robin egg we found this spring? At times, the sky is just that color.

I've used six rolls of film in my camera already. I should have some awesome pictures to show you when we get home in two weeks.

closing—a word or phrase that signals the end of the letter, followed by a comma

See you soon,

signature—the writer's name

Cal

BUSINESS LETTER

Depending on the prompt, you could be asked to do any of the four types of writing in a business letter. Combine what you know about essay writing with the format of a business letter.

Read the prompt below. Then see how the elements of persuasive writing were used in the business letter that follows.

Prompt

Imagine that a neighborhood park has become the hangout for a gang of older teenagers. The park is now littered with soda cans, beer bottles, cigarette butts, and other kinds of trash. Write a letter to a city council member asking that the park be cleaned up and made safe. The following is the information you will need for your inside address. William T. Collins, Councilman, City Hall, 12345 Council Avenue, Westtown, Washington 98007

body—the paragraphs that state the purpose of the letter

closing—a word or phrase that signals the end of the letter, followed by a comma

5431 Park Lane
Westtown, Washington 98007
January 2, 19—

heading—writer's address and the date

William T. Collins, Councilman
City Hall
12345 Council Avenue
Westtown, Washington 98007

inside address—the name, title, firm, and address of the person you are writing to

Dear Mr. Collins:

greeting—tells whom the letter is to, followed by a colon

Are you aware of the condition of Smith Park? Would you want your children to play there? I don't think so. My mother won't let me play there. Recently, a gang of older teenagers has taken over the park. They are using it for a hangout. They scare the younger children and shout insults at adults. Broken bottles, cans, and trash litter the area. I am asking for your help in cleaning up the park and making it safe.

The park has become an eyesore in the neighborhood. I think the city would be embarrassed if visitors to the city drove by and saw the peeling paint and litter. If the city council would provide the funds for clean-up materials, the people in the area are willing to do the work for nothing. We need your support.

Once or twice a week, the police chase the gang away. But the gang is back before the police are around the corner. In other parts of the city, officers walk around to keep gangs from hanging out in public places. You could suggest that the city assign an officer to patrol the Smith Park area on foot.

I am inviting you to come to Smith Park and see for yourself what has happened to this once beautiful park. If you look at the park through the eyes of the people living here or of visitors to the city, I'm sure that you would agree that something needs to be done to save the park.

Sincerely,

Shauna Powers

Shauna Powers

signature—the writer's name

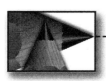

LETTER TO THE EDITOR

A letter-to-the-editor prompt will require you to write a formal letter stating your opinion on a subject. Depending on the prompt, you could be asked to do any of the four types of writing.

Read the prompt below. Then notice the elements of both narrative and descriptive writing in the response that follows.

Prompt

Reading for fun has been a concern in your school for the past year. This year teachers at your school have started an afterschool program for children. With the help of high school and parent volunteers, a book club has been formed. Children choose their own books to read. Then for an hour, three afternoons a week, they read to themselves, each other, or the volunteers. Every month the group has a reading party. Write a letter to the editor of your school newspaper that expresses your feelings about this program. Include a story from your experience that supports your opinion.

body—the paragraphs that follow the greeting

closing—a word or phrase that signals the end of the letter, followed by a comma

heading—the day, month, and year the letter is written

November 28, 19–

greeting—tells whom the letter is to, followed by a colon

Dear Editor:

I think the afterschool Celebrate Reading Book Club is a great idea. Many students at Longfellow Elementary go home after school and plop down in front of the TV set. They watch talk shows that deal with adult subjects or cartoons that are mindless. But our teachers have come up with a fantastic solution for afterschool boredom. The Celebrate Reading Book Club has doubled in size since it began in September. Kids are spreading the word about the fun we have. Then others come to check it out.

In September, 40 students brought their favorite books to share. We now have our own book-club library of over 200 titles. Each boy and girl chooses a book to read. Some of us read to each other. Some read to themselves or the volunteers. What is really great is the fact that our teachers say our reading has improved.

Last week, several kindergartners who don't read came to the book club. They were excited just to sit with some first and second graders and listen. These nonreaders have a love of books too. If the program continues, one day they will be able to share books with younger children who can't read at the Celebrate Reading Book Club.

Sincerely,

Anthony Crivaro

Anthony Crivaro
6789 Calhoun Street
Kansas City, MO 64151

signature—the writer's name and address

REPORT

Some writing tests may require you to write a report based on a situation and notes provided in the prompt. Since a report is informational, it normally involves writing to explain.

Read the prompt and notes below. Then see how the elements of writing to explain were used in the report on the next page.

Prompt

Your social studies class has been studying Mexico. For your class project, you have decided to write a report about plants and animals found in Mexico. You have done some research by reading several books and magazine articles. The notes you took about this subject are listed to the right. Organize the notes into a written report. Be sure to

- keep in mind that you are writing the report for your social studies class.
- rearrange the notes before you start to write.
- include all the information from the notes in your report.

Notes

Life in the high plateaus

—prairie dogs   —coyotes
—lizards   —rattlesnakes

Forests in southern mountains

—mahogany   —walnut
—rosewood

Cactus in the dry plateaus

Life in the mountains

—bears   —deer
—mountain lions

Pine and fir trees in the northern mountains

Unique trees such as sapodilla in southern mountains

—milky sap   —sap used in chewing gum

Fish

—tuna, swordfish, sardines, shrimp, oysters, abalone
—sold in Mexico and around the world

Variety of plants in southern jungles (warm and moist)

—orchids, azaleas, poinsettias
—vines and ferns
—wild coffee, vanilla, cocoa bean plants

Life in the southern jungles

—jaguars, opossums, monkeys, snakes (boa constrictor)
—quetzal (the bird of paradise)

Tough grass on the high plains

Life in jungles and along the coast

—flamingos, herons, parrots, hummingbirds

continued

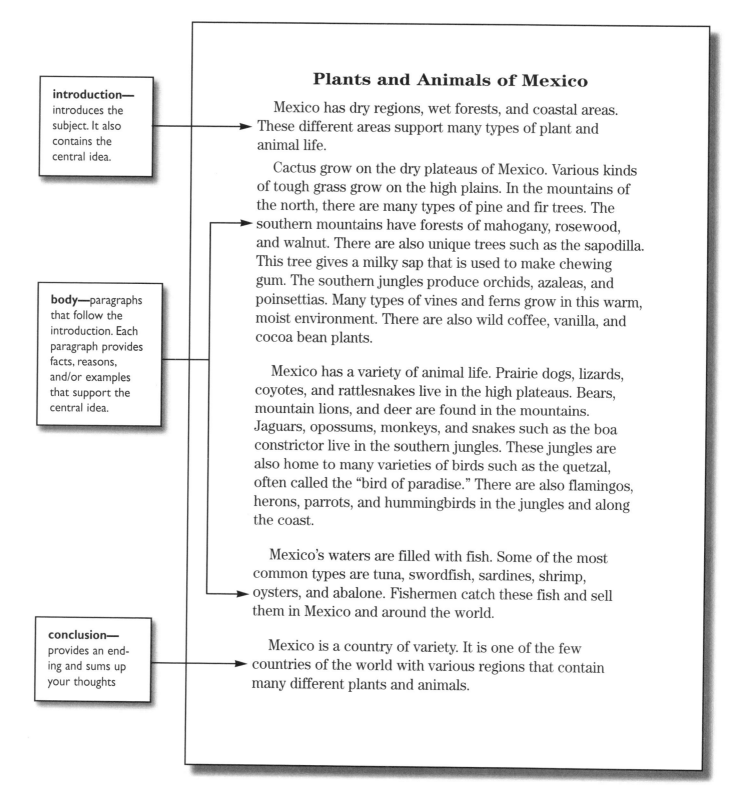

introduction— introduces the subject. It also contains the central idea.

body—paragraphs that follow the introduction. Each paragraph provides facts, reasons, and/or examples that support the central idea.

conclusion— provides an ending and sums up your thoughts

Plants and Animals of Mexico

Mexico has dry regions, wet forests, and coastal areas. These different areas support many types of plant and animal life.

Cactus grow on the dry plateaus of Mexico. Various kinds of tough grass grow on the high plains. In the mountains of the north, there are many types of pine and fir trees. The southern mountains have forests of mahogany, rosewood, and walnut. There are also unique trees such as the sapodilla. This tree gives a milky sap that is used to make chewing gum. The southern jungles produce orchids, azaleas, and poinsettias. Many types of vines and ferns grow in this warm, moist environment. There are also wild coffee, vanilla, and cocoa bean plants.

Mexico has a variety of animal life. Prairie dogs, lizards, coyotes, and rattlesnakes live in the high plateaus. Bears, mountain lions, and deer are found in the mountains. Jaguars, opossums, monkeys, and snakes such as the boa constrictor live in the southern jungles. These jungles are also home to many varieties of birds such as the quetzal, often called the "bird of paradise." There are also flamingos, herons, parrots, and hummingbirds in the jungles and along the coast.

Mexico's waters are filled with fish. Some of the most common types are tuna, swordfish, sardines, shrimp, oysters, and abalone. Fishermen catch these fish and sell them in Mexico and around the world.

Mexico is a country of variety. It is one of the few countries of the world with various regions that contain many different plants and animals.

On Your Own

Now it's your turn to respond to a prompt from one of the other types of writing tests. Choose one of the following prompts.

Prompt

Report

Your science class has been learning about endangered animals. For your class project, you have decided to write a report about elephants. You have done some research by reading several books on elephants. The notes you have taken are listed at right. Organize the notes into a written report. Be sure to

- keep in mind that you are writing the report for your science class.
- rearrange the notes before you start to write.
- include all the information from the notes in your report.

Notes

Only survivor of their group of mammals

Hunted for sport

1989—609,000 elephants

Hunted for meat

Today—less than 25,000

Elephants' land taken up by farms and cities

Hunted for ivory tusks

—worth a lot of money

—used to make art

1979—1.3 million elephants

Land ruined by fires

Today land set aside for national parks (also called reserves)

—Africa and Asia

—not enough to save elephants

Prompt

Business Letter

You recently bought a model car kit that was missing several parts. The store is out of the particular model that you bought. Write the company a letter asking them to replace the missing parts. Include reasons for your request. The following is information you will need for your inside address. Toys That Last, P.O. Box 654, River Valley, Minnesota 55439.

Prompt

Friendly Letter

You have moved to a new town. Write a letter to your best friend where you used to live. Describe your new school and any friends you have made.

Prompt

Letter to the Editor

The city has just passed a law that requires children under 13 to be home by 9 p.m. unless they are with an adult. Write a letter to the editor of your local newspaper that expresses your opinion about the new law.

COMMON PROBLEM AREAS
IN ESSAY WRITING

It is easy to make mistakes in writing. This is especially true if your test is timed. This chapter deals with common problems found in essays written by students your age. Read through each problem area. Then complete the activities that follow. Learning how to avoid these problems now can result in a better essay—and a better test score.

PUNCTUATION

Every sentence needs a punctuation mark at the end. Some sentences need punctuation marks in the middle or at the beginning too. These marks make your ideas clear for the reader. Without them your writing is just a jumble of words. Read each rule and the examples below. Then complete the activity at the end of the section.

Period

- Use a period at the end of a sentence that makes a statement or command.

    EXAMPLE   *Carlos hit the baseball over the fence.*

    EXAMPLE   *Please close the front door.*

- Use a period after an initial in a name.

    EXAMPLES   *Barbara J. O'Neill   T. Henry Boyd*

- Use a period at the end of an abbreviation.

    EXAMPLES   *Ms.   Dr.   Ave.   Inc.*

Question Mark

- Use a question mark at the end of a direct question.

    EXAMPLE   *Will it be sunny tomorrow?*

    EXAMPLE   *Where is Charlotte?*

> **As You Write...**
> Look at every punctuation mark. Is a punctuation mark needed there? If so, is the correct mark used? Punctuation should match the thoughts you've expressed.

Punctuation continued

Exclamation Mark

- Use an exclamation mark at the end of a word, phrase, or sentence to show a strong feeling.

EXAMPLE *Wow!* (word)

EXAMPLE *Happy birthday!* (phrase)

EXAMPLE *You scared me!* (sentence)

Comma

- Use commas to separate items in a series.

EXAMPLE *Trine plays softball, volleyball, and basketball.* (words)

EXAMPLE *Geoff jumped out of bed, ran down the stairs, and opened the front door.* (phrases)

- Use a comma between a city and state.

EXAMPLE *Mary grew up in Greenwich, New York.*

- Use a comma between the day and the year.

EXAMPLE *I was born September 13, 1988.*

- Use a comma after the greeting in a friendly letter.

EXAMPLES *Dear Mom,   Dear Li,*

- Use a comma after the closing in all letters.

EXAMPLES *Sincerely,   With love,   Yours truly,*

- Use a comma before the connecting word in a compound sentence. Common connecting words are *and, but,* and *or.*

EXAMPLE *Kelly wants to go fishing, but she won't bait the hook.*

EXAMPLE *Su Ling has a new cat, and she named it Snowball.*

Punctuation continued

- Use a comma to set off the exact words of a speaker from the rest of the sentence.

EXAMPLE *Linus said, "I hope it doesn't rain today."*

EXAMPLE *"Dinner is ready," Dad announced.*

EXAMPLE *"Group one stand by the door," said Mrs. Smith, "and group two stand by the windows."*

- Use a comma to set off introductory words and phrases and words of direct address.

EXAMPLE *However, we may need your help.*

EXAMPLE *Mike, the phone is for you.*

Colon

- Use a colon after the greeting in a business letter.

EXAMPLES *Dear Mrs. Jenkins: Dear Councilman Peters:*

- Use a colon before a list.

EXAMPLE *Mr. Links has three cars: a Ford, a Chevy, and a Buick.*

Apostrophe

- Use an apostrophe in contractions.

EXAMPLE *Maria isn't going to school today.*

- Use an apostrophe to show ownership.

EXAMPLE *Jo Beth gently touched the dog's paw.* (singular)

EXAMPLE *The boys' clubhouse was hidden by the shrubs.* (plural)

As You Write...
Read each sentence to yourself.
Wherever you pause in the sentence,
there should be a punctuation mark.

Quotation Marks

- Use quotation marks to set off a speaker's words. In almost all cases, punctuation is set inside the quotation marks.

  EXAMPLE   *Mother yelled, "Come in the house right now!"*

  EXAMPLE   *"Bill, please take this home," said Mrs. Kelk.*

- Use quotation marks for the title of a short work (song, poem, short story).

  EXAMPLE   *We sang "Swing Low, Sweet Chariot" in music class.*

  EXAMPLE   *I wrote a poem called "The Wind."*

  EXAMPLE   *Jake chose to read the story called "The Black Dog of Willow Creek."*

Directions: The following sentences don't have punctuation. Rewrite the sentences using the correct punctuation. Use the punctuation rules for reference.

1. Did Ms Owens check Aleesas homework

_____

_____

2. Calvin paid for Timmy Hal and Kerry to go to the movies

_____

_____

3. M J McCloud was born May 18 1982

_____

_____

4. Melanie grew up in Seattle Washington

_____

_____

5. Wow I just finished a great short story called The Pumpkin Autumn

_____

_____

6. Mrs Jones is absent today the substitute said but she will return tomorrow

_____

_____

7. Marcus caught the ball dribbled to the basket and made the shot

_____

_____

8. Carrie is going to the park and she invited me to go along

_____

_____

9. Sam has four dogs Skipper Shadow Murphy and Mutt

_____

_____

10. Billy you did a great job

_____

_____

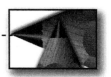

CAPITALIZATION

Everyone knows that the first word of a sentence and the pronoun *I* are capitalized. But there are other times that capital letters are needed. Read each rule and the examples below. Then complete the activity at the end of the section.

- Capitalize the first word in a quotation.

    EXAMPLE   *Mother said, "The winter months are my favorites."*

- Capitalize the names and initials of people.

    EXAMPLE   *Robert T. Sanchez*

- Capitalize the first word in the greeting and closing of a letter.

    EXAMPLES   *Dear Aunt Sue,   Very truly yours,*

- Capitalize titles used with names. Do not capitalize titles if they are used alone.

    EXAMPLES   *President Franklin D. Roosevelt   the president*

- Capitalize abbreviations of titles and organizations.

    EXAMPLE   *Dr.* (doctor)

    EXAMPLE   *YMCA* (Young Men's Christian Association)

    EXAMPLE   *NOW* (National Organization of Women)

- Capitalize the first and last words of a title and every important word in between.

    EXAMPLES   *The Sign of the Beaver   Nothing Is for Free*

As You Write...
Capitalize "firsts"—the first word in a sentence, in a quotation, and in the greeting and closing of a letter.

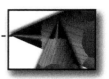

- Capitalize the names of the days of the week, months, and holidays. Do not capitalize the seasons.

| EXAMPLES | *Wednesday*   *February*   *New Year's Day*   *summer* |

- Capitalize the names in geography.

EXAMPLES	*Mount McKinley, Andes Mountains* (landforms)
	Ledges State Park, Washington Monument (public areas)
	Earth, North Star (planets and heavenly bodies)
	Empire State Building, Astrodome (buildings)
	Lake Erie, Amazon River, Pacific Ocean (bodies of water)
	Asia, Europe (continents)
	Bosnia, Great Britain, Mexico (countries)
	South Dakota, Arkansas (states)
	Alberta, Yucatan (provinces)
	Seattle, London (cities)
	Pennsylvania Avenue, Main Street, Route 66 (streets, roads, highways)

Common Capitalization Mistakes

Capitalize	Do Not Capitalize
Mother helped me tie my shoe. (used as a name)	My *mother* helped me tie my shoe.
Councilman Williams visited our neighborhood. (title used with a name)	The *councilman* visited our neighborhood.
I went to the fair in *August.* (name of a month)	The fair is held every *summer.* (a season)
We go to *Lake Michigan* every year. (name of a specific lake)	We go to the *lake* every year.
We traveled through the *West* during our vacation. (a section of the country)	We traveled *west* for our vacation. (a direction)

 **Directions:** Rewrite the sentences using the correct capitalization. Use the capitalization rules for reference.

1. haley and i visited niagara falls in new york.

_____

_____

2. the worst day of my life was on a spring day in april.

_____

_____

3. last wednesday i walked down holcomb avenue to johnson memorial park.

_____

_____

4. i can't get used to people calling my mother councilwoman saunders.

_____

_____

5. the park avenue pta asked r. j. raskins to run for president.

_____

_____

6. mexico and canada are both parts of north america.

_____

_____

7. marie asked henry, "do you know where the book is?"

_____

_____

PARTS OF SPEECH

Every word in our language fits into one of eight groups. These groups are called *parts of speech*. Read each rule and example below. Then complete the activity at the end of the section.

Nouns

- Common nouns name any person, place, thing, or idea.

  EXAMPLES *dog   park   game*

- Proper nouns name a specific person, place, thing, or idea.

  EXAMPLES *Rover   Ranger Park   Monopoly*

Use the following rules when forming plurals for nouns.

How to Form Plurals of Nouns

Rule	Example	
Most noun plurals are made by adding an -s.	girl/girls	toe/toes
Nouns ending in s, x, ch, and sh are made plural by adding -es.	bus/buses fax/faxes	church/churches dish/dishes
Nouns ending in a consonant and y are made plural by changing the y to i and adding -es.	family/families spy/spies	country/countries
Nouns ending in a vowel followed by a y are made plural by adding -s.	toy/toys decoy/decoys	cowboy/cowboys
Nouns ending in a consonant followed by an o are made plural by adding -es.	hero/heroes echo/echoes	tomato/tomatoes
Nouns ending in a vowel followed by an o are made plural by adding -s.	video/videos patio/patios	radio/radios
Irregular nouns are made plural either by changing the spelling or by remaining the same.	child/children wife/wives deer/deer	mouse/mice leaf/leaves

Directions: Rewrite the sentences, choosing the correct plural from the parentheses to fill in the blank. Use the noun rules for reference.

1. The (child, children) were waiting on the corner.

   _____

   _____

2. Last night we had chicken, (potatoes, potatos), and carrots for supper.

   _____

   _____

3. The Boy Scouts built new (benchs, benches) in the park.

   _____

   _____

4. I helped the neighbors pick (cherrys, cherries) on Saturday.

   _____

   _____

5. My sister caught fourteen (fish, fishes).

   _____

   _____

6. Tamara received (bookes, books) for her birthday.

   _____

   _____

7. Six (countys, counties) held fairs during August.

   _____

   _____

Pronouns

- A pronoun takes the place of a noun. Some pronouns can be singular or plural depending on the words they replace.

- A subject pronoun shows who or what does something. Subject pronouns are *I, we, you, he, she,* and *they.* If you use two or more pronouns that include *I,* write *I* last.

- An object pronoun shows to whom or to what something is being done. Object pronouns are *me, us, you, them, him,* and *her.* If you use two or more pronouns that include *me,* write *me* last.

Directions: Rewrite the sentences, choosing the pronoun that correctly fits in the sentence. Use the pronoun rules for reference.

> ### As You Write...
> Check your pronouns to be sure they reflect the noun correctly. Also, if you use two or more pronouns that include *I* or *me,* write *I* or *me* last.

1. (She, Her) sang a solo at the concert.

   _____

   _____

2. Do (he, they) want to come with (we, us)?

   _____

   _____

3. I noticed that (he, him) has a new coat.

   _____

   _____

4. (I, me) am invited to attend the opening of the new store.

   _____

   _____

5. Ben and Sarah wanted to share (his, their) cookies with Jolie.

_____

_____

6. Sally fell off the bike and broke (her, his) leg.

_____

_____

7. All the Boy Scouts worked on (his, their) merit badges.

_____

_____

8. Larry drew a picture and hung (him, it) on the wall.

_____

_____

Adjectives

- An adjective describes a noun or pronoun, telling what kind, how many, or which one.

  EXAMPLE   *The **enormous** spider crawled up the side of the house.* (what kind)

  EXAMPLE   ***Eight** students passed the writing test.* (how many)

  EXAMPLE   ***This** dog is Kathy's.* (which one)

- The adjectives *a*, *an*, and *the* are called articles. *A* is used before words beginning with a consonant sound. *An* is used before words beginning with a vowel sound.

  EXAMPLE   *A man knocked on the door.*

  EXAMPLE   *An orange tastes better than **an** apple.*

> ## As You Write...
> Use adjectives to provide readers with the same mental picture that you have. The adjectives should appeal to the readers' five senses when possible.

- An adjective sometimes compares two nouns. The ending *-er* is added to one-syllable adjectives. The word *more* is used before many adjectives with two or more syllables.

  EXAMPLE   *Tim is **shorter** than Billy.*

  EXAMPLE   *Social studies is **more interesting** than science.*

- An adjective sometimes compares three or more nouns. The ending *-est* is added to one-syllable adjectives. The word *most* is used before many adjectives with two or more syllables.

  EXAMPLE   *Jupiter is the **largest** planet.*

  EXAMPLE   *Beau is the **most lovable** dog.*

Directions: Complete the following paragraph using an appropriate adjective in each blank. Use the adjective rules for reference.

The _____ frog sat on the _____ lily pad.

Suddenly, there was a/an _____ splash behind the frog. It

was _____ than any splash the frog had ever

heard. The _____ water almost knocked it off the

lily pad. The _____ frog turned around and saw the

_____ creature ever to live in the _____

pond.

Verbs

- An action verb shows action or tells what a noun is doing.

    EXAMPLE *Mick **walked** home from school.*

- A linking verb links a noun to another word. The linking verbs are *is, are, was, were, am, be,* and *been.*

    EXAMPLE *Molly **is** the only girl on the football team.* (The word *is* links *Molly* to *girl.*)

- A helping verb comes before the main verb and helps tell what the action is or when the action takes place. Helping verbs are *has, have, had, will, could, should, would, do, did, may,* and *can.*

    EXAMPLE *Elena **has finished** her homework.*

- A singular verb should be used to show the action of a singular noun. A plural verb should be used to show the action of a plural noun.

    EXAMPLE *Connie **lives** on Maple Lane.*

    EXAMPLE *Connie and Mindy **live** on the same street.*

- Verbs show when the action happened. An *-ed* is added to regular verbs to form the past tense. Future tense is often formed by adding the helping verb *will* to the present tense. The chart on the next page shows the irregular verbs that form tenses by not changing at all or by respelling.

    EXAMPLE *Yesterday Terry **played** with his new dog.* (The action happened in the past.)

    EXAMPLE *Today Terry **plays** with his new dog.* (The action happens in the present.)

    EXAMPLE *Tomorrow Terry **will play** with his new dog.* (The action will happen in the future.)

As You Write...

Compare your subjects to their verbs. Make sure both are either singular or plural. If you don't know whether a noun is singular or plural, try saying it in your mind using one or two different verbs. Decide which "sounds" right and choose that one.

Common Irregular Verbs

Present		Past		Past with a helping verb
am		was		been
begin		began		begun
blow		blew		blown
break		broke		broken
bring		brought		brought
catch		caught		caught
choose		chose		chosen
come		came		come
cut		cut		cut
do		did		done
draw		drew		drawn
drink		drank		drunk
drive		drove		driven
eat		ate		eaten
fall		fell		fallen
fly		flew		flown
give		gave		given
go		went		gone
lay		laid		laid
leave		left		left
lie		lay		lain
make		made		made
read		read		read
ride		rode		ridden
ring		rang		rung
rise		rose		risen
run		ran		run
see		saw		seen
sing		sang		sung
speak		spoke		spoken
take		took		taken
teach		taught		taught
wear		wore		worn
write		wrote		written

Directions: Complete the sentences. Use the correct form of the verbs in parentheses to fill in the blanks. Use the verb rules for reference.

1. José _____ ill when he answered the door.   (look)

2. Jaime will _____ for the owner of the dog next week.   (search)

3. Tulips usually _____ in the spring.   (bloom)

4. Mary had _____ a letter to her brother.   (write)

5. Jerry and Sean _____ together last year.   (work)

Adverbs

- An adverb is a word used to describe a verb by telling *where*, *when*, or *how*. Adverbs often end with *-ly*. Common adverbs are *not*, *never*, *very*, and *always*.

    EXAMPLE   *Lily waited **outside** for Sasha.* (where)

    EXAMPLE   *Stephen slipped **quietly** into his chair.* (how)

    EXAMPLE   *Lucy **never** eats meat.* (when)

Directions: Complete the sentences. Fill in the blank with an adverb that answers *where*, *when*, or *how*. Use the adverb rules for reference.

1. _____ Tammy asked Kim to play on the soccer team. (when)

2. Chad yelled _____ when his brother made a touchdown. (how)

3. Farley _____ takes his sister to the movies. (when)

4. Bobby looked _____ for his dog. (where)

5. Aleesa painted the wall _____. (how)

Prepositions

- A preposition is a word used to show the relationship of a noun or pronoun to another word. The preposition is the first word of a phrase that ends with a noun or pronoun.

  EXAMPLE *The dog jumped **onto** the chair.*

  EXAMPLE *A car raced **down** the street.*

Common Prepositions

about	around	by	like	outside	under
above	at	during	near	over	underneath
across	before	for	of	past	until
after	behind	from	off	since	up
against	below	in	on	through	with
along	beneath	inside	onto	to	within
among	between	into	out	toward	without

ACTIVITY

Directions: Rewrite the sentences, choosing a preposition to fill in the blank. Use the preposition rules for reference.

1. Tickets _____ the talent show went on sale at noon.

2. An owl hooted _____ my window.

3. I found a box of old clothes _____ the attic.

4. "Let's build the clubhouse _____ the barn," suggested Larry.

5. Zina was surprised by the houses that were damaged _____ the storm.

Conjunctions

- A conjunction is a word that is used to connect words or groups of words. Common conjunctions are *and, after, because, before, but, for, nor, or, since, so, until, when, where, while, yet.*

    EXAMPLE   *Millie **and** I collected shells.* (two nouns connected)

    EXAMPLE   *The crow squawked **and** flew away.* (two verbs connected)

    EXAMPLE   *Benji phoned home, **but** no one answered.* (two sentences connected)

    EXAMPLE   *I won't be home on Saturday **because** I have to play soccer.*

    EXAMPLE   *Mom needed more sugar, **so** I went to the store.*

Directions: Rewrite the following pairs of sentences as one using a conjunction to connect words, phrases, or sentences. Use the above rules for reference.

1. Thomas wanted cucumber in his salad.
   He wanted onion in the salad too.

   _____

   _____

2. Many customers like Mrs. Chang.
   She is very friendly.

   _____

   _____

As You Write...
Look closely at your conjunctions, such as *and, or, but,* or *since.* The wrong conjunction can change the meaning of the sentence.

3. The doctor told Liz to stay in bed.
   She got up as soon as he left.

   _____

   _____

4. Katy can read some English words.
   Katy can write some English words.

   _____

   _____

5. Mr. Riley was ill today.
   We had a substitute teacher.

   _____

   _____

Interjections

- An interjection is a word or phrase used to express a strong emotion. It is followed by an exclamation mark or a comma.

    EXAMPLE ***What a great day!*** *Ted hoped it would never end.*

    EXAMPLE ***Hey,*** *drop that stick!*

ACTIVITY   **Directions:** Rewrite each sentence using an interjection in the blank. Use the above rule for reference.

1. _____ ! The water's too deep, and I can't swim!

2. _____ , bring that paper here now!

3. _____ , did you make that all by yourself?

TRANSITIONS

Transitions are words that help the reader follow the order in which events happen. *First, then,* and *finally* are examples of transitions.

Mickey wanted to make a special dinner for her friend. **First** she made a grocery list. She checked the cupboards and wrote down what she needed. **Next** Mickey picked up her purse, got into her car, and drove to the store. **Then** she walked through the aisles picking up what was on her list. **Finally** Mickey paid for her groceries and headed home.

Directions: Write a short paragraph of your own. Use transition words to show the order of events.

_____

_____

_____

_____

_____

_____

_____

_____

_____

SENTENCE STRUCTURE

A sentence has a subject and a verb, and it expresses a complete thought. We use sentences every day when we speak, when we read, and when we write. There are three major problem areas when writing sentences.

> ### *As You Write...*
> Make sure your sentences are clear and well-written. Make sure that punctuation shows where one thought ends and the next

Fragment

- A sentence fragment does not express a complete thought. It is missing the subject or the verb.

EXAMPLE	*Opened the door for Grandma.* (no subject)
CORRECTED	***I*** *opened the door for Grandma.*

EXAMPLE	*The fuzzy caterpillar on a stick.* (no verb)
CORRECTED	*The fuzzy caterpillar* ***crawled*** *up the stick.*

EXAMPLE	*Enough players for a game of stickball.* (not a complete thought)
CORRECTED	***We have*** *enough players for a game of stickball.*

Run-on

- A run-on sentence is one that contains two or more sentences without correct punctuation.

EXAMPLE	*Jimmy played baseball, he hit a home run.*
CORRECTED	*Jimmy played baseball. He hit a home run.*

Rambling

- A rambling sentence is one that goes on and on.

EXAMPLE	*Mary had a birthday party and her friends came and she received many presents and her favorite present was a kitten.*
CORRECTED	*Mary had a birthday party. Her friends came and brought her many presents. Her favorite present was a kitten.*

Directions: Correctly rewrite each fragment, run-on, or rambling sentence. Use the sentence-structure rules for reference.

1. Dylan climbed the tree and he was really high and he called his mother and she was very impressed and she went to get her camera to take his picture.

   _____

   _____

2. Today portabella mushrooms popular everywhere.

   _____

   _____

3. The baby-sitter knocked at the front door she came in.

   _____

   _____

4. Played checkers with Uncle Will and Aunt Mabel.

   _____

   _____

5. Everybody loves Dr. Mitchell she treats all kids like they're old friends.

   _____

   _____

6. Waited for the movie to begin.

   _____

   _____

SENTENCE COMBINING

Sentence combining makes one longer sentence out of two or more shorter sentences. These longer sentences can make your writing more interesting and easier to read.

EXAMPLE	*Katrina likes pizza. Katrina likes macaroni. Katrina likes muffins.*
COMBINED	*Katrina likes pizza, macaroni, and muffins.*
EXAMPLE	*Marcus ate hot lunch. Maddie ate hot lunch.*
COMBINED	*Marcus and Maddie ate hot lunch.*
EXAMPLE	*Butch and his father went skiing. They went skiing yesterday.*
COMBINED	*Butch and his father went skiing yesterday.*
EXAMPLE	*Lizzie turned the key in the lock. The door opened easily.*
COMBINED	*Lizzie turned the key in the lock, and the door opened easily.*

Directions: Read the following pairs of sentences. Correctly write a combined sentence for each pair.

> ## As You Write...
> Listen to your sentences. Are they all the same length? If so, break up sentences that are too long. Combine short, choppy sentences. Remember that a combined sentence should still have the same meaning as the smaller sentences.

1. Gretchen wore an dress.
   The dress was ancient.

   _____

   _____

2. Elephants are huge animals.
   Hippopotamuses are huge animals.

   _____

   _____

3. Dusty had a lot of fleas.
   We bought flea shampoo and gave Dusty a bath.

   _____

   _____

4. The guide showed me the beaver's den.
   The guide showed Sue the beaver's den.

   _____

   _____

5. Serena found oak and maple leaves.
   Serena found acorns and pinecones.

   _____

   _____

6. We wanted to go to the beach.
   The beach was too far away.

   _____

   _____

7. The children baked the sugar cookies.
   The children decorated the sugar cookies.

   _____

   _____

8. People drove their cars through the intense snowstorm.
   People drove their cars cautiously.

   _____

   _____

TEN TIPS FOR QUICK REVISION

More than likely, you won't have a lot of time to rewrite your test essay. That's why it's important to be able to decide quickly what to fix. As you read through your finished product, think about the following elements. Be ready to revise if necessary.

❑ Reread your central idea carefully. Make sure it indicates the exact subject of your paper.

❑ Make sure your body paragraphs are clear. If you find a sketchy detail, add an additional line of explanation in the margin.

❑ Look for words you might have omitted. Use a caret (^) to indicate where a word should be inserted. Then write the word below the caret.

❑ Listen for natural pauses. Insert commas where necessary.

❑ Scan for capitalization. Make sure all words at the beginning of sentences, as well as any proper nouns, are capitalized. Cross through the word and write the capitalized version above.

❑ Look for misspelled words. If you find any, neatly draw a line through the word and rewrite the correctly spelled word below the misspelled one.

❑ Check to see that your sentences end in the appropriate punctuation (period, question mark, or exclamation point).

❑ Make sure you have included transitions where needed. Again, use a caret (^) to indicate where a transition should be inserted. Then write the transition above the caret or in the margin.

❑ Look for words you might have written twice. Make a neat line through one of them.

❑ Listen for awkward wording. Fix this by neatly crossing through the word or phrase. Then place your revision above or in the margin.

Below is an essay to explain. Notice how the writer revised her writing using the tips listed on page 62.

The job of fifth‿grade class president involves a number of
-

tasks. This person will need certain qualities to handle them.

The class president takes daily attendance‿plans class parties,
,

collects money for field trips, and makes daily announcements.

He‿will need to be organized in order to handle the work in class
∧
or she

and the responsibilities of president.

The
~~the~~ president will need to be creative ~~if~~ because he or she plans class

parties. Math skills also will be important since the president

collects money for field trips.

The president makes announcements over the loudspeaker.

grammar
Therefore, he or she will need a clear voice and good ~~grammer~~ ∧
.

math
Organized. Creative. Good in ~~Math~~. A good speaker. These

are all qualities that a person should look for when voting for a

fifth-grade class president.

TEST-TAKING TIPS

Each chapter in this book offers tips and strategies that will help you in a writing-test situation. Here are some additional tips.

1. Begin by quickly looking at all the prompts. This will help you see what the test is about. It will also tell you how many essays you need to write.

2. Read each prompt carefully. Locate any key words or phrases that will help you find the subject of the essay.

3. Once you know the subject of the essay, organize your thoughts about the topic. Use graphic organizers if they help you get your thoughts down quickly. Then begin writing.

4. Note the time you have for each essay. Use a few minutes at the beginning for prewriting. If you have time left over at the end, use it for revision. Use most of the time for writing the essay. Note: Don't stop writing to revise. It is more important to finish your essay than to revise what is already written.

5. If you feel nervous before the test, try this. Close your eyes. Take several slow, deep breaths. Then spend a few minutes trying to relax your mind.